Writer Inc.

Starting and Growing Your Writing Business

Marnie Hughes

Table of Contents

Printer/Scanner

Internet Connection

Office Supplies

Chapter 3: Business Matters

Types of Business

Registering Your Business

Business Insurance

Media Insurance

Conducting Market Research

Creating a Business Plan

Chapter 4: Service Offerings: What Will You Write?

What Kind of Work Is Out There?

Project Management

Website Management

Research

Email Marketing

Niche Writing

Editing

Charity Village List of Charities

Suggested Cold Calling Script/Intro Email Format

Online Writing Job Sites

Chapter 8 Notes

Chapter 9 Notes

Business Networking Groups

Appendix B: Templates and Samples

Chapter 3: Business Plan Table of Contents Sample

Chapter 4: Competitor Analysis Worksheet

Chapter 5: Customer Identification Worksheet

Chapter 7: Income Statement Template

Chapter 7: Cash Flow Template

Chapter 8: Marketing Plan Table of Contents Sample

Introduction

If you're reading this book, chances are you are one of two kinds of people. One—you're a writer. Or at least you want to be a writer, and something in the pit of your stomach tells you that you have what it takes to become one. Two—you want to start a business. In this case, you might be motivated by the freedom and independence that self-employment brings. Or perhaps you've lost your day job and are struggling to find employment. Does any of this sound like you?

While both are good reasons to get started, which one do you think will serve you as you keep going? Will you still have the drive and passion to write a year from now, even if you work on projects that are less than exciting? Will you still feel the freedom a year from now when you end up working weekends to catch up on the accounting side of the business?

Of course, it's difficult to know what will drive you in a year, but what you must realize is that for all the romance behind the notion of starting your own business or becoming an author, there is also a great deal of hard work and determination. If that scares you, then perhaps you should set this book down and pick up a compelling novel. If the thought of hard work or adversity is a mere shoulder shrug to you, then read on. I can share with you what I've learned to help smooth some of the bumps in the road.

With over ten years of growth and success in my writing business, I can honestly say it's a journey I wouldn't trade for anything. I have learned so much standing on the shoulders of genius. I have met incredible professionals who have become valued clients and close friends. I've written some of my best work that made me proud of what I do. I've been able to be there for my family at times when a 9 to 5 job would not have allowed it. And now, I have one of the most incredible opportunities of all—I can share what I've learned and teach others how to do what I did. I am driven by the chance to see even one other person realize this dream and reach the level of joy and contentment that I have attained. If you're ready to get started, turn the page and let's begin!

Chapter 1: Do You Have What It Takes?

Writing has been an integral part of my life for as long as I can remember. When I was a child, it was common to find me sitting on the windowsill in my bedroom, writing stories or journal entries on rainy days. I found comfort in putting pen to paper and made a point of bringing my notebook everywhere with me. In those days, writing letters longhand (gasp!) was quite common, and through my school I had been introduced to pen pals from across the globe. What a thrill it was for me to write about my little country life while learning about the fascinating world in Korea and Germany. The pen pal exercise was really a chance for those students to practise their English, but for me it was a peek into other cultures.

Those early years are how writing became ingrained in my daily life. It never occurred to me that this could be something I could pursue as a career. In fact, it wasn't until much later, when I was taking a break from my career, that the concept of writing as a job presented itself.

During the final months of my second pregnancy, my husband and I decided that the logical course of action would be for me to stay home with our two children. The cost of daycare and commuting amounted to almost as much as my salary at the time, so it made sense that I should spend the time raising my children and not be much worse off. Little did I know that I really wasn't wired for the "stay-at-home mom" job.

When my second child was about four months old, I found myself often feeling disconnected and dissatisfied. I had always had a career with lots of outside stimulation and responsibilities that resulted in recognition and commendations when the job was well done. I loved my kids, but how was I going to do this?

One of the things that helped me turn the corner was a book entitled *The Well-Fed Writer* by Peter Bowerman. Peter had a way of describing the writing business in such a casual, obtainable way that I believed it was something I could do. A lot has changed in the thirteen years since reading that book, but the message still resonates today. Websites and social media are prominent now. This book will share with you what writing opportunities exist today and how to tap into them. It will also talk about being adaptable to what may come in the future. The world of communication is changing so rapidly that you need to pay attention and find your place on an ongoing basis.

Writing Skills

Have you ever written an email or letter? Have you prepared a resumé or cover letter? Did you attend elementary school and high school? If you answered "yes" to these questions, then chances are pretty good that you have what it takes to be a writer. It is a myth that you need to be a graduate of an English Literature program in order to be a good writer. The level of skill you need depends on where you plan on executing your craft, but to start a writing business and to get good-paying, quality projects to work on only requires basic knowledge of the language, such as spelling, grammar, and syntax.

If you plan on writing a great novel or appealing to highly technical communities, your abilities will need to be more finely tuned. You will need to speak the language of the audience you serve. If this is your goal, it is still achievable and may involve getting additional training to proceed.

Storytelling is an important part of writing. Any kind of writing. Rather than just being confined to novels, telling stories is a wonderful way to get a message across. Stories are easier to read, are relatable, and often invoke emotion in the reader. The point is to get the message to the reader in whatever way possible. Telling a story is one of the most effective ways to make that happen.

Adaptability Skills

Methods of communication have evolved significantly in the past decade. There is every reason to believe that they will continue to change and develop as people demand more convenience and connectivity. We once wrote letters that went into a mailbox. This morphed into using email as a quick and efficient method of connecting. Then social media platforms sprang up everywhere for you to choose whatever method you wanted to stay in touch and share information with friends. Today, sending a text message to your mobile device is one of the quickest methods of communicating. Perhaps tomorrow it will simply be a matter of saying or thinking something and having it magically reach the individual it's meant for!

Through all of this, there have been writers. And they have had to adapt to the medium of the time. Messages went from lengthy handwritten letters to abrupt and tightly edited text messages. The key is paying attention to what is happening and matching your talent and service with the needs you identify. Your greatest tools are your willingness to learn and your openness to new ideas. To be a competent writer, you must be a prolific reader. Keep topping up your tool kit with information gathered from all manner of sources. Read from many sources, not just from your favourite blogs. Read various types of books—novels, business, poetry, the classics. Flip through magazines and newspapers. Listen to audio books and podcasts. Fill yourself with ideas, information, and creative stimulation to expand what you are capable of offering to your readers.

Separating Business from Pleasure

Since you're just getting started, I will assume that you plan to work from home. One of the challenges of setting up a business in your home is to separate the work environment from personal space. You may not be able to set aside an entire room for your writing business, which means you'll have to find a way to focus on work when necessary, and separate your business from your personal life. This will become more critically important if you are working on a project that pays by the hour, because your client will not pay for the half hour you "stepped out" to do a load of laundry. Establish clear lines in your space and time to minimize confusion between what is classified as "work" and what is classified as "personal."

Handling Isolation

Working as a writer involves a great deal of time alone with a keyboard and your thoughts. For large tracts of time, you will be by yourself, so the ability to handle isolation is critical. How do you handle being alone? Do you enjoy the solitude or do you fidget in desperate need of human contact? For the most part, you will have control over your schedule, which means that you can slot networking or in-person meetings between the blocks of quiet writing time. If being alone bothers you, think of places where you can write in public, such as libraries and coffee shops. Didn't J.K. Rowling pen much of the Harry Potter series in a coffee shop? Take the time to understand your limits in this regard and plan on how to overcome them.

Research Skills

Research is the gathering of data, information, and facts for the advancement of knowledge (http://en.wikipedia.org/wiki/Research_-Definitions). You will need to develop your research skills to be able to adapt to what the industry requires of writers at any given time. You will also need to learn how to conduct research in order to write on topics with which you have little or no experience. Online resources are vast, and much of the research you will need to do can be conducted on the Internet. There are other sources, however, and they are worth investigating. Libraries and experts are valuable resources that help to round out your information supply chain.

Organizational Skills

Keeping yourself organized does not have to be a daunting task. Knowing where everything is, however, will save you time as you get busier. Have you ever lost your keys and spent hours looking for them, only to discover they were in the pocket of the jacket you wore yesterday? You'll soon discover that time is precious, so being organized is your ticket to saving time.

When I first started, I kept a binder that contained a spreadsheet listing each of the projects I was working on and their due dates. I would manually record what milestones I had reached on each project, and then tick off the Complete box when it had been submitted to the client. There are numerous digital options that can do the same thing. My current tool of choice for managing simultaneous projects is Asana (asana.com). It is a free online project management program that enables me to set up projects and tasks within those projects. Each task is assigned a deadline, and I can invite others to view the task as well if they are collaborating with me on the project. Asana also includes several other features, such as the ability to add files and documents related to the project.

Your work world will also involve a physical space, and you'll want to keep that organized. Setting up a separate file for each client and a method for keeping track of where they are in your priority system will save you endless hours of aggravation. Once a job is complete, the file will be put away into a historical filing system until you decide it can be discarded. And do make a point of going through the old files and getting rid of them. Notes and research from a project you did last year on a topic you will not likely do again should be discarded. Believe me, you don't want to be overrun by your files, no matter how organized they are!

Customer Service Skills

When you purchase a product or service, how do you expect to be treated? At the very least, with respect and courtesy, right? Imagine that your customers expect the same. Although writing may seem like an isolated calling, you will be dealing with clients on a regular basis. Your initial meeting will give them that valued first impression of you, and this is your opportunity to show them what kind of person you are. Do you have a sense of humour? Are you "all business" and do you stick to the facts alone, or do you lighten it up a bit with non-work conversation? How does the customer respond to your approach? One of the most valued skills in your tool kit should be the ability to read and respond to people. If a customer is panicked and in a hurry, you could counter with a calm and reassuring approach. If the customer wants to chat about their new dog and anything but the project, you could gently steer the conversation back on track. The point is, you will need to interact with people all the time. Whether they are customers, colleagues, or vendors, be conscious of your ability to provide exceptional customer service.

Selling and Marketing Skills

As I mentioned, Peter Bowerman, author of *The Well-Fed Writer*, was very influential in getting me started in the writing business. One of the skills he outlines in his book is how to do cold calling. For me, this was the biggest obstacle. I simply couldn't work up the nerve to pick up the phone and talk to a complete stranger about possibly hiring me. I did it, though, using the techniques he suggested, but every time, I broke out in a cold sweat and lamented that this was a part of the job. I knew I'd never get any clients if it continued to be such a stress for me, so I began to look for other ways to find work.

What I quickly learned about was the power of word of mouth. I told everyone I knew that I was now a writer and working on corporate projects as well as magazine articles. This, of course, has morphed into an explosion of opportunity on the Internet, but at the time, it was about getting work for corporate communications such as brochures and newsletters, or submitting articles to various magazines. The coming chapters will provide more details, but keep in mind that selling and marketing skills will need to be an essential part of your tool kit if you're going to make a go of your own writing business. With the wide variety of marketing tactics available to you, there is a very good chance that you'll find one to fit your comfort level.

These are some of the key things to keep in mind while you consider your writing career. And remember, a healthy dose of self-confidence will go a long way in helping you over the challenges when they come your way.

Chapter 2: Getting Started

Once you've evaluated your strengths and weaknesses, if you still think you have what it takes to start your own writing business, congratulations! The first step really is all about being confident enough in yourself to BELIEVE you can achieve this goal. What will you need to get started?

Full Time or Part Time

Your personal situation is unique; therefore, your decision regarding how much time to dedicate to your business will be customized to meet your needs. When I started my writing business, I was a new stay-at-home mom with a husband who was paying the bills. I enjoyed a certain level of freedom in terms of time and money. I wasn't obligated to pay for the groceries every week because that was taken care of. This put me in a "pressure-free" position to start my writing business. My full-time job and obligation at the time was to take care of and raise my children. I still consider that to be my primary responsibility, but I am now able to balance the time spent between the two jobs because the kids are older and more self-sufficient. Not everyone enjoys that luxury.

If you're planning to start a writing business, you likely fall into one of two camps. Either you are dissatisfied with your current employment and want to try something else, or you are out of work and need to earn an income. In the latter case, making money *now* will seem more urgent, and committing to a full-time effort in writing might make sense. But know this—establishing yourself as a competent writer will take time. You should not depend upon the remote possibility of getting rich quick. Many people who are looking for full-time employment may want to start up a freelance writing business on the side while continuing their search. If this makes sense to you, then go for it. If your only choice is to chase the dream full time, understand that there will be a ramp-up period during which you are developing your skills and network of potential clients.

For those who are gainfully employed but want to start a writing business for the fulfillment of living that lifestyle, I would recommend approaching it on a part-time basis while you are getting established. Knowing where your next paycheque is coming from and being certain you can continue to keep a roof over your head and food on your table will alleviate a lot of stress. If you jump ship from your current employment because you are certain you will be a famous writer within weeks of leaving, you may just be setting yourself up for disappointment. On the other hand, if this has been on your mind for a long time and you've saved up enough money to have a six-month "cushion" to survive while you go full bore into your business, then you're heading toward success. That level of forethought is a saving grace when things get scary and uncertain. It also suggests that you have the capacity to plan your way to a goal. This will be invaluable as you move forward.

Let's be honest. Starting a business costs money. It may not be a lot in terms of actual cash outlay (if you already own a computer and a desk to work on, and have Internet access, the cost is close to nothing), but it will require a lot of your time. Factor this into your plan when you are getting started. If you've chosen to stay at your full-time job, then understand that starting your business will be conducted on your personal time. Get your family and friends on board, and explain to them what you're doing. Not only will you find that you have a built-in cheering section, but they will understand when you have to miss something due to commitments with developing your business. Strive to find balance between work and play. It is possible to reach this harmonious place, so be sure to make a conscious effort to do so. For example, I have a set start and end to my work day and do not answer my business phone outside that time. My family knows that when my door is closed or my headphones are on, I am working and am not to be disturbed. I do, however, make time for special events or activities when needed, even if they occur during the workday.

Workspace

If you are serious about starting a business, then it should appear that way to those around you. Many entrepreneurs start out in a home office or a corner of the basement, or some other specifically designated space where they will go to work. In the early days, I had a couple of filing cabinets and a table in the spare room. Having a place where I could close the door to have quiet while working or making phone calls was important to me. My family knew that the closed door meant I was working and could only be interrupted if it was very important. Setting these boundaries early gets everyone else on the same page as you are, and it reminds you of how important the work is. You've made the decision to embark on this venture. Now, you have to be disciplined to see it through.

Even if you don't have a separate room in which to work, designate a table or corner that you can clearly identify as your working space. Use an in-basket or standing file to identify it if you need to, but create something distinctive to let everyone know that this is where the writing business happens. If possible, make it off limits for any other activity, so you subconsciously know that every time you sit at that table, it is time to go to work.

Tools

Chair and Desk

In your space, you'll need a comfortable place to sit and a surface on which to work. It is worth investing in a good-quality chair, as you will be spending a great deal of time in it. Office supply stores are fantastic for providing a wide selection of ergonomic chairs at several price points, so you're bound to find one that works for you. Avoid using a dining room chair or folding chair as these are simply not ergonomically friendly, and you could wind up with chronic back pain. Many professionals engaged in sedentary work include regular chiropractic or massage therapy visits in their routine. Maintaining a healthy back is much easier than repairing a damaged one.

Your table or desk needs to be at the right height to work with your chair. Having your shoulders hunched up while trying to type is not fun. The pain can last a very long time if you permit carpal tunnel to take hold. Carpal tunnel syndrome is an ongoing tingling or numbness in your wrists that is often accentuated by occasional sharp pain. It is a progressive condition caused by the compression of a key nerve in your wrist. While it is not a foregone conclusion that this condition will result from hours at the keyboard, you should consider taking appropriate precautions to avoid it. If symptoms do present themselves, be sure to have them checked out by a physician.

A piece of advice here—writing for a living means you'll be doing a lot of sitting. There are some ways around this, such as a standing desk, or walking and dictating into a recording device. If you're like most writers, however, you will be sitting for large chunks of time. I've compiled a list of suggested exercises (see Chapter 2 Notes in Appendix A) to help minimize the damage that can result from excessive sitting. Keep in mind that you can only be productive (and engage in your other interests) if you are well. Take care of yourself and you will be productive *and* able to enjoy yourself!

Computer

A desktop or laptop computer will be the primary tool of your business. The options on the market are extensive and the available features vary a great deal. Something new comes out every year, so technology can often get dated quickly. It all boils down to personal preference. However, it is strongly recommended that you select a computer with the most memory possible—not just the hard drive capacity, but the actual RAM memory that dictates computer speed. It's not that your document file sizes will be that big, but the higher memory will improve your online speed. With the constant opening of photos, videos, and other large files, maximum memory will give you optimal performance.

Generally, you would choose between a laptop and desktop computer. Arguments can be made for either—the laptop is portable so you can write anywhere, and the desktop has a larger screen for editing or viewing multiple documents simultaneously. A tablet isn't necessarily conducive to doing extended amounts of writing, but it may be a tool you would want to include in your arsenal.

Start with clearly identifying what you plan to do with the computer. Will you be using the computer solely for surfing the web, word processing, and sending emails? Do you intend to use the computer to create websites and graphic designs? Are you going to create videos or animation? Will you run an online store? Each of these activities will have a minimum requirement in terms of performance. Some activities will need more storage or processing power, while others will demand a more powerful video card or larger screen.

Next, determine your budget. The price range for a general-use computer can start as low as C$400. A computer at this price point may not have all the features you're looking for. You'll likely adjust your budget or narrow down your feature requirements until the two reconcile. Then, check out a few stores or online sites to get a sense of where you might get the best value for your dollar. Once you've done your research and are content with your findings, make your selection and purchase. Prices and functionality change quickly, but in order to get started, you'll need to make a decision so you can get to work. I've worked with the same laptop for six years and it has served me well for both my writing and online needs. (See the web links in Chapter 2 Notes of Appendix A to help you choose the right computer for your specific needs.)

Printer / Scanner

Depending on what kind of projects you are working on, it is very likely that most of your submissions will be done by email or file transfer. You may question the need to have a printer. Again, it comes down to personal preference and working style, but I have found that occasionally printing a page I'm working on is extremely helpful, especially in the editing process. As well, there will be some people who want to see a hard copy of a piece in a meeting where a computer is not available. Such requests may be diminishing, but the needs for a printer do still exist, and it is definitely worth investing in one. Printers are usually inexpensive and can often be bundled into a package along with the computer that you purchase. Always shop around to get the best deal.

Many printers also double as flatbed scanners. This can be of use if you are given a printed form to fill out and return. There may be times when you have made written changes on a printed document and you need to show it to someone right away. Simply scanning and emailing your handwritten notes takes only a matter of minutes. On the business side, scanning receipts or relevant printed documents and saving them along with everything else related to a project will enable you to keep everything in one place. This is a real time saver.

Internet Connection

Much of the research conducted by writers occurs online. You'll need a high-speed Internet connection to facilitate this. Service providers will vary depending on the region you live in, but it's worth doing some comparison shopping. There is enough competition in this space that you may be able to take advantage of package or bundle deals, such as adding Internet service to your existing phone or cable line.

Office Supplies

Equip yourself with typical office supplies such as pens, paper, paper clips, stapler and staples, file folders, filing cabinets, highlighters, sticky notes, envelopes, and stamps. The list goes on and will vary depending on your office management style.

I find that two of my most-used office supply items are a notebook and pen. It may sound a little old school, but I still like to jot notes as I'm talking on the phone to a client. I also choose to keep my "Top 4" to-do list items handy, so rather than have them in the task list on my smartphone, I keep them with me in this notebook.

These items are my suggestions for what you'll need to get your business started. You may have other ideas, and you will definitely be adding to the list as you go along. You will find that having immediate access to certain reference materials such as a thesaurus, dictionary, and style guide quickly become daily tools of the trade. At first, however, much of the information you'll need can be found online or at your local library. Try to keep your initial costs to a minimum while you are still in the "getting started" phase. This will reinforce good business habits as you move forward.

Chapter 3: Business Matters

In this chapter, we'll take a look at the different types of business set-ups that you could engage in, although you will likely start out as a sole proprietor working just for yourself. You should understand the differences so you can make decisions about business structure as your company grows.

Types of Businesses

In Canada, there are three primary business structures: sole proprietorship, partnership, and corporation.

A **sole proprietorship** is an entity that is owned and operated by an individual. That individual is solely responsible for all activities of the business. This means that all the money made goes to the individual, and all expenses are charged to the individual. The finances become a part of your personal income tax calculation, so hiring an accountant to help you properly calculate this is a very good idea. Any legal issues relating to the business will also be attributed to the individual.

A **partnership** puts two or more individuals in a co-owner position. Each of the partners is responsible for parts of the business, and this is best handled with a well-written partnership agreement. Each partner should be clear about their responsibilities, both in activity and contribution, as well as financial and legal liability. A proper partnership agreement is a legal document and should always include an exit strategy. As excited as you may be in starting a partnership, they almost always dissolve at some point; therefore, if you are both prepared with how that will be handled, it is easier to keep the business elements detached from the emotion of the situation.

A **corporation** is a legal entity separate from the individuals who own or work for the company. This means that any financial or legal obligations of the company will be attached to the corporation, not to the individuals.

There is a cost to setting up a corporation, and there are certain rules you'll need to adhere to, such as assigning a board of directors, maintaining articles of incorporation, and having audited financial statements each year. This may make sense if the principal of the company no longer wants to be financially responsible for the activities of a number of employees. Legal and financial advice will be required to formally set this up and maintain the proper documentation.

Registering Your Business

The rules may be slightly different from province to province, but in Ontario it is very simple to register your business and make your company "official." There is a valuable resource in the province of Ontario called ServiceOntario, which provides all the details you need to get started (see Chapter 3 Notes in Appendix A for a link to the ServiceOntario website).

First, decide what your Business Name is going to be. It's a good idea to come up with two or three ideas in case your first choice has already been taken. Make sure that your selected business name accurately reflects what you do. It should be unique and easy to remember. You'll need to have ServiceOntario do a search for your business name before you can proceed with registration. Both the name search and registration must take place prior to you receiving your Master Business License. This is the official document that you will print out and display in your office or keep with your important documents for use in official situations, such as for your accountant or bank.

If you anticipate making in excess of $30,000 a year, you will need to register for HST (Harmonized Sales Tax) if you live in Ontario. You can do this on the Canada Revenue Agency website (see Chapter 3 Notes in Appendix A for a link to the HST registration web page). You may wish to register even before you reach the $30,000 mark so that you can take advantage of tax credits. This means that the HST on allowable expenses can be deducted from the HST you collect from clients, giving you a bit of an advantage. There is also a Quick Method for calculating quarterly HST payments. Before proceeding with registering for HST, though, you may wish to discuss this with your accountant, as you might not have enough deductions to make it worthwhile. On the other hand, you can present an image to your clients that you are a large enough company to charge HST, which may give you more credibility.

Record keeping is an integral part of running a business. The Canada Revenue Agency website offers a lot of how-to information on keeping track of income and expenses, including a guide on keeping records and what documents you'll need to keep and produce in the event of an audit (see Chapter 3 Notes in Appendix A for a link to the business records web page).

Business Insurance

Your business has many assets, such as vehicles, office equipment, and you. It may make sense for you to protect your business from potential risks. Different types of insurance to consider include insurance of owners and key employees, insurance for business property and earnings, liability insurance, accounts receivable insurance, and health insurance.

Since you are just starting out, if something were to happen to you, the business would simply fold and cease to exist. Once you're established, however, it may be possible that your business could continue without you. If you've grown your business to include subcontractors and a substantial client list, it is possible that someone could take the reins and continue running the business after you're gone. But if you are the only person working on projects, and you are the creative force behind all the writing, once you are no longer here, the talent that is your business is gone as well. It makes sense to have a conversation with your accountant or lawyer to determine what makes the most sense for your situation. If you already have life insurance with a disability component, your family will be taken care of, which for many is the most important consideration.

Media Insurance

As a writer, you may want to consider getting liability insurance that will cover you in the event of such things as libel claims. Error and Omissions coverage can often be customized for your specific situation. Ask your insurance broker for more information on the type of liability coverage that makes sense for you.

Conducting Market Research

Market research is the process of gathering information that will help increase your awareness of how people will respond to your service offerings. The point of doing market research is to equip yourself with the information you need to make informed business decisions about start-up, growth, product, price, and promotion. It will help you understand your customers and their preferences, identify opportunities to grow, recognize economic shifts, and monitor the competition.

To conduct research, you can use simple methods such as observation, experimentation, or surveys. You can also review statistical data found in libraries, industry associations, and government departments. Researching your competition will also assist in highlighting what it is that potential customers are looking for in a product/service provider. (See Chapter 3 Notes in Appendix A for a link to the Canada Business Network website and its guide to market research and analysis.)

Creating a Business Plan

Some people think that a formal business plan is a critical part of any business. However, a sole proprietor may exaggerate the detail and magnitude required in a business plan. Your plan can be encapsulated in a few pages if it outlines exactly what activities you plan to engage in, how you will charge for the services you offer, how you will find customers to buy what you're selling, and your goals and milestones to gauge your success. Ideally, a business plan is a guideline that helps you to move in the right direction, but it is a document that will evolve as your business moves forward. In many cases, your business plan is only viewed by whoever will be giving you money, such as an investor or partner.

If you're looking for some ideas as to what to include in a formal business plan, you can find a link to a downloadable template for start-ups in Chapter 3 Notes of Appendix A. Also see a sample business plan table of contents in Appendix B.

Included in a standard business plan are both the marketing plan and the financial forecasts. These documents should be developed as you decide how you are going to make your business successful. These topics will be discussed in later chapters.

Chapter 4: Service Offerings: What Will You Write?

What Kind of Work Is Out There?

Writing is needed just about everywhere. Here is an extensive (but not exhaustive!) list of the types of writing projects you can do. While looking over the options, think about what appeals to you and what you are capable of writing. Many of the items on this list require additional training, so if they interest you, then consider what training you'll need in order to be successful. As you view the list, you'll see several items for which you may feel qualified. Try to narrow the field to just a few project types so that you can develop your skills and experience, making your services of greater value to potential customers.

One consideration is to tap into your previous experience. For example, if you've worked in a restaurant before, you may have a knack for describing dishes to make them tantalizing to customers and can write menu copy. Or perhaps you can write restaurant reviews for a local newspaper or magazine. If you were a teacher in a past life, writing training materials or textbooks might be just right for you. Take a look at the list here and see what types of writing projects you can pursue.

- **Ad copy** – agencies, marketing departments of companies, large companies with in-house advertising departments; small businesses that need a professional but can't afford the cost of an ad agency
- **Anniversary materials** – corporations, banks, associations, churches, cities that have a significant anniversary coming up: you could write an organizational history, profiles of significant players
- **Annual reports** – more complex, not usually for beginners
- **Articles** – business or trade journals
- **Blog posts** – research and write
- **Brochures** – corporate, small business, professionals; organizations, seminar promoters, hospitals, medical groups, educational institutions, community and government agencies, churches, non-profits

- **Case Studies** – success stories to illustrate how companies have helped clients
- **Collateral materials** – order forms, spec sheets, invitations for corporations, ad agencies, PR firms
- **Critical reviews** – write reviews for local newspapers or magazines about restaurants, theatre, dance productions, books
- **Direct mail** – results-oriented specialty: write copy that pulls; requires study as this takes special skill; choose a specialty, e.g., financial, consumer, business-to-business, subscription sales, fundraising
- **eNewsletters** – businesses, organizations
- **Fund-raising materials** – if you have no portfolio or past experience, this is a great place to volunteer and develop your samples, e.g., colleges, universities, hospitals, zoos, museums
- **Greeting cards** – a huge market with billions of cards sent every year; can specialize
- **Instructional/Training materials** – HR departments, marketing departments
- **Newsletters** – corporate / associations
- **Policy and procedures manuals** – safety, quality, environmental
- **Political campaigns** – research, policy statements, mailers, websites; connect with a local political group
- **Product catalogues/ Product sheets** – brief descriptions of products, or full-page specs and details of products; retail, industry, corporations, ad agencies, photographers, graphic designers
- **Proposals** – requires special training/experience; write for non-profit organizations, fund-raising consultants
- **Public relations materials** – press kits, educational materials, speeches, newsletters
- **Researching** – use online resources, libraries; work for a marketing team, publisher, law firm, government agency
- **Resumés / Cover letters** – employment agencies
- **Retail promotions** – brochures, flyers, point-of-sale displays
- **Sales letters** – corporate, small business

- **Sales presentations** – marketing research and product information; multimedia
- **Scripts** – videos, podcasts, radio ads, televisions ads; work for TV/cable stations, ad agencies, or independent producers
- **Social media posts** – Facebook, Twitter, LinkedIn, Google+, etc.
- **Speeches** – CEOs, politicians
- **Technical writing** – manuals, reports, instructions; very specialized for manufacturers, governments, IT companies
- **Telemarketing scripts** – powerful sales techniques; you'll need to learn and research to become proficient at this
- **Training materials – instruction sheets/guides, forms for participants, course outlines**
- **Travel writing** – for magazines, newspapers, or associations
- **Website copy** – research and write
- **White Papers** – authoritative reports to educate industry customers

I'm assuming that you love to write, which is why you've decided to set up your own freelance writing business. I've learned, however, that there is a lot more opportunity out there than just writing. In fact, you may find that the demand for your writing skills is often accompanied by other client needs. What other services and skills can you bring to the business that will complement your writing and enhance your customer's satisfaction? Here are a few suggestions based on my experience:

Project Management

I worked with a small business owner who was essentially a "one-man band" and had to do everything himself. Being a smaller company, he had no marketing department or sales team, but he was extremely good at what he did—software development in a niche market. He was planning to attend an industry trade show where he was already well known, and he wanted to produce a brochure that he could hand out to prospects. Initially, he contacted me to write the brochure copy, but once we discussed his overall needs, he realized that there was more to producing

31

a brochure than he thought. As we discussed the format, design layout, content, online companion piece, and so on, he grew pale. This was simply out of his comfort zone, so he asked me to take care of it.

Because I had already established relationships with graphic designers and printers, as well as web developers, I was able to quickly put together a team that could produce what he wanted in the time frame that he requested. Had it not been for my organizational skills and confidence in my colleagues, I would not have attempted to quote on this project, and I would have lost out on a lucrative assignment. It made all the difference to my client that he was able to concentrate on his strengths while preparing for the trade show, and feel confident that the marketing tool he wanted would be produced to his satisfaction. Everyone wins.

If you're going to delve into project management, make sure that you have the organizational skills to handle multiple tasks. Having the right tools is critical. I've used an online program for several years that enables me to set up projects and tasks within each project. There are several features that include setting due dates, inviting colleagues to collaborate, and uploading documents to the project. See Chapter 4 Notes in Appendix A on the project- and time-tracking tools that have helped keep me organized. Chapter 6 discusses these useful and powerful tools in more detail.

I've also found using project management software helpful for my own business activities. I've set up a project called Communication Artistry, under which is my website, blog, bookkeeping, marketing activities, and so on, so I know how much time I'm spending on different tasks related to my business. This helps me with my planning.

Website Management

Many small business owners need more than just the copy for their website. I work with web developers and designers in partnership to develop websites, and this provides the client with the final product that they can manage for themselves. In many cases, however, business owners are discovering that maintaining a website with regular updates can be very time-consuming. You may wish to consider offering ongoing service to these clients by providing regular updates and uploading them to their website. Many websites are built on a content management system (CMS), which enables an average individual to make updates to their site. It would be a great advantage to learn a CMS such as Joomla, Wordpress, or Dot Net Nuke in order to offer this service to clients. Of course, having this skill means that you are better equipped to manage your own website as well.

Research

It goes without saying that to complete most writing projects, a certain level of research is required. Sometimes, you may offer only research as a service. It is not unusual for one of your clients to be a colleague or fellow writer in need of research services. In fact, many of the customers I've served over the years have been writers. We have collaborated on projects or passed along referrals for prospects that would be better served by another writer. In these cases, the client did not need polished copy; they only needed some research done. It sounds simple, and it can be, but be clear about what the customer is expecting before you jump in. If the topic is obscure, you may find it difficult to gather information. Research is conducted in a variety of ways, not exclusively through a Google search. If you plan to offer just research as a service, make sure you know what methods work best for you and set parameters on what types of topics you will look into. Every job will be unique, and what the client needs will vary. You may be asked to provide a bullet list of facts for a brief blog post, or several pages of detailed research for a feature article.

In addition to online research through search engines, visit your local library where you can access reference works such as government publications, historical documents, books, and periodicals. You can also

33

conduct first-hand research by observing people and situations. Subject matter experts are also an excellent resource and can be interviewed in person or by telephone.

Email Marketing

Clients who require online marketing services also often need writing services. This leads to two opportunities: 1) writing the copy for the email/eNewsletter to be sent out, and 2) sending out the email for the client. Some may regard the sending activity as more of an administrative assistant task, but I have learned that customers want solutions. If you are able to provide the copy for the eNewsletter, and you have the online experience to actually set up and send that email, then you provide more value for your clients than someone who just provides the copy. If this is something you'd like to consider, then think about whether you have enough online experience and savvy to offer advice, and provide this service to your clients. If not, what training do you need to be able to provide these additional services? Two popular email programs are MailChimp and Constant Contact (see Chapter 4 Notes in Appendix A for links to these websites). Both programs are well equipped with instructions to guide you through creating and sending email campaigns. They are also set up to record data such as opens, bounces, and click-throughs—all valuable information to measure the success of your email campaign.

Niche Writing

Pay close attention to the industry you are planning to serve. You may have years of experience as an engineer, for example, in which case you'd be well qualified to write technical reports or manuals to serve that industry. If you decide to provide specific niche services (e.g., technical writing), exactly what skills will you need to be successful in that field? Can you tap into your experience from a previous job that would benefit your target market? What training could you acquire that would put you above your competition?

Editing

Almost 50 percent of my business involves some form of editing. Clients either have written something that they aren't satisfied with and want it professionally edited, or they have older materials that they would like to repurpose and use in a new way. I have often had a client provide an article that they like and want to use as inspiration to produce their own blog post. Naturally, you would never copy someone else's work, but there are generally facts or ideas that can be incorporated into your new piece. In some cases, clients such as book publishers, authors, agents, teachers, and professionals have produced something that simply needs a second pair of eyes to critically review.

Keyword Research

Much of what you write may be destined for the online world, meaning people will be searching for it by using keywords. Take some time to learn the skill of conducting keyword research, and to identify the tools available that can enhance your ability in this area. Google offers an easy-to-use keyword suggestion tool that enables you to identify the estimated number of searches for any given keyword phrase, both on a global and regional level. This tool will take your initial keyword request (e.g., "red shoes") and offer suggestions as to what other keyword phrases visitors might enter (e.g., "red leather shoes" or "red shoes toronto"). Go through the suggested list and select the keyword phrases that are relevant to you. You can then download this selected list to a spreadsheet program, where you can collect and sort data related to these keywords (see Chapter 4 Notes in Appendix A for links to the Google AdWords and Wordtracker websites).

Consultation

You may be called upon prior to doing any work or even quoting on a job to provide advice to a potential client as they plan to prepare a newsletter, website, or other marketing initiative. It's one thing to provide some friendly advice; however, it's another thing entirely to provide consulting services. Clarify early on what the customer is looking for and expecting. Make it clear up front what fees you charge for consulting services or whether you provide a certain amount of consulting free at the commencement of a new project. Ensure that expectations are clearly written out and discussed to avoid confusion.

A Note About the Competition

There are many writers out there. Some are very talented and prolific, others not so much. The good news is that there is plenty of need for quality writing. The bad news is that some very unskilled people also claim to be professional writers. How you present yourself is extremely important because your prospect will make a decision on very little information in just a few seconds. In an upcoming chapter, we'll touch on how to market yourself, including how to develop your own professional website and blog.

Take a long, hard look at your competition. Are they located in your geographic area, or are they all over the world? What are they offering that you aren't? If they offer the same or similar services, what will make you stand out and become the writer of choice for new customers? (See Appendix B for a sample competitor analysis worksheet.)

Consider the scope of services that you offer as compared to your competitors. Will social media be included with your service offerings? Will you write blog posts, and will you also upload them to the website for the client? Will you set up an editorial calendar for clients to follow, or will you execute the plan for them as well by managing social media postings, email marketing, and website updates?

This chapter has tried to illustrate the vast scope of writing opportunities. The skills needed for each project will vary, meaning that you may need to enhance your current skills with training and research to better service the clients you wish to target. It is strongly recommend that you choose just a handful of writing services and focus on excelling in those areas. Spreading yourself too thin will simply result in you providing mediocre writing to a wider range of people. It will also mean that your chances of repeat business will be greatly diminished.

Chapter 5: Finding Work

There are writing opportunities everywhere. Some may not be immediately apparent, and not all of them are online. The trick is to find where the paying work is and go after it. Yes, there are a lot of other writers out there, but you can be sure that there is also a need for a lot of writing. I've always found that there's enough business to go around for someone who is skilled with words and who is willing to put in the work. So, where do you look?

Make Your Own Work

I'm sure that's not what you had in mind when you picked up this book. Let me explain. You are just starting out. You may have samples of letters, articles, or blogs that you've written, and these can be used in your portfolio. Suppose there is an area you'd like to concentrate on, such as ad copy, for example; what do you do if you haven't written an ad before? Flip through a publication containing ads and choose one that you feel is poorly written or that can be improved. Then do it. Get creative and rewrite the ad the way you think it could read. Put that in your portfolio.

Once you've assembled a few writing samples in various categories that you'd like to work in, build a website that details your skills and services, and that also provides a portfolio of some of your work. This is your online resumé, so have some fun and show your creative side.

How to Build a Basic Website

If you have never built a website or feel less than technically capable, do not fear. There are a vast number of websites and videos online that will teach you how to do it. To create a website, you'll need three things: a domain name, website hosting, and website-building software. A detailed description of the steps to follow in building a website can be found in Chapter 5 Notes of Appendix A.

Tap Your Network

When you are in the beginning stages of your writing business, your best starting point is to reach out to your existing network. Tell family, friends, colleagues, and anyone you engage in conversation that you have started a writing business and are actively seeking new clients. Announce it on your social networks with a link back to your website. Consider offering special discounts to first-time clients so they can try out your services.

Non-Profit Organizations

If you're just starting out and having trouble getting those higher-paying assignments because you have a limited portfolio of samples, why not do some pro bono (free) work for a non-profit organization? Many non-profit charities would welcome the expertise you can offer while creating articles, brochures, newsletters, or online content. And it would also be a great opportunity for you to show your writing skills and develop your portfolio.

Not for profit is not limited to charities such as the Cancer Society or Alzheimer's. Look at local hospitals, zoos, museums, schools, senior's centres, and so on, for opportunities to share your writing expertise. As you move forward in your writing career, you may consider the non-profit sector as an area where you focus your professional efforts. There are many charitable organizations in need of competent writers. For listings of Canadian non-profits, visit the Charity Village website (see Chapter 5 Notes in Appendix A for a link to the website).

Corporations

Every business needs writing of some kind. In many cases, individual staff members are expected to do the necessary writing. Unfortunately, in today's environment, every employee is typically overloaded with the tasks they are already responsible for. Adding writing jobs on top of that workload may become too onerous. In such cases, it makes sense for the company to contract out certain writing tasks, including business letters, speeches, technical manuals, brochures, newsletters, ads, blogs, websites, and social media posts. So where do you look to find these opportunities?

There are a few ways to locate businesses that may be in need of your writing services. At this stage, you will have considered what type of writing you want to do, and therefore you've determined who your ideal client(s) would be. Check out your local library for business directories that will provide details of such organizations. You might also consider trying Scott's Directories (a free trial is available) to locate the type and size of business you are targeting. Online, you can search through LinkedIn for specific companies or industries to see what professionals are registered. LinkedIn is ideal for locating the names and positions of decision makers at the companies you wish to approach. You can then reach out to them with an offer. (See Chapter 5 Notes in Appendix A for a cold-calling script and/or introductory email format. See Appendix B for a Customer Identification Worksheet template.)

Online

You've likely heard the term "content is king," which means that the content you find on a blog or website is the most important thing online. Content not only includes the words, but also the pictures, video, and audio elements that you see and hear every day. Your writing services might be needed to write the content for a website or blog, but consider that your skills might also be needed to write the script for either the video or podcast.

There are many websites that list potential writing opportunities. These sites vary a great deal, and the types of jobs you'll find may or may not suit your skills and interests. Take a look at some of the online writing job sites listed in Chapter 5 Notes of Appendix A to see if these might be a good source of work for you.

The suggestions offered here are by no means exhaustive, so I hope that you will be inspired to come up with your own creative ideas on where to find writing work.

Chapter 6: Discipline and Time Management

Not everyone can be self-employed. How do you find out if you have what it takes to work for yourself? One of the best ways to find that out is by taking a look at your current habits and behaviours. If you are working right now, do you meet deadlines that are set for you? Are you able to set your own deadlines and milestones, and meet them? Be honest with yourself when you answer these questions. Think about who is ensuring the job gets done on time. Is it your drive and sense of commitment that enables you to meet your goal, or are you supervised by someone else who has to provide motivation?

Discipline: Getting the Work Done

When working on multiple projects, it can be difficult to stay on track. It is very easy to dive into the enjoyable and interesting website project when you know that the challenging technical article has a more urgent deadline. Having the discipline to set priorities for various projects is the key to getting the work done and satisfying your customer.

There are tools you can use that help a great deal with keeping you on track. Scheduling and project management programs help keep you organized, and they include the ability to insert due dates into each task, invite colleagues to collaborate on tasks, and allow for notes and files to be attached to each task and project. Alerts can be set on your calendar to make sure that certain milestones are met. I use a combination of methods to help keep me on task. I set up projects and tasks in Asana (www.asana.com), and set due dates for the items that have a finite duration. Some projects are ongoing and are billed monthly. The program sends me an email each day to tell me what's due and how soon. I use this as a guideline to lay out my daily tasks. I have found it most helpful to review the current tasks and projects at the end of the day in order to set up my work for the following day. This helps me to "hit the ground running" first thing when my mind is at its freshest.

In addition, I use a tool called Toggl (www.toggl.com), which is a time-tracking program. I have a desktop icon that allows me to click Start and Stop when working on projects. This is handy when there are several tasks on my plate for a given day, and I'm bouncing back and forth between them. It's also a real eye-opener when I hit Start at the beginning of my email session, only to discover I've spent an entire hour pulled into that non-billable abyss. Toggl is particularly useful for recording time for projects that are billed by the hour. This gives you a detailed account of your activities in the event that your client wants backup data.

Discipline: Treating It Like a Business

You may have wanted to start your own business for the freedom of working on only those projects that appeal to you, and for the freedom of defining your own time schedule. To make your dream a reality, it will take hard work, and lots of it. If anyone tells you that starting and growing your own business is a piece of cake, either they're lying to you or they're hoping you'll sign up for whatever it is they're selling!

To manage your own business, you will need to keep careful track of all the income and expenses that the business generates. These figures will need to be tracked diligently in case you are audited, but more importantly so that you can hand them over to your accountant for tax filing. You will need to set budgets and cash flows so that you know how your business is progressing, and you don't over-extend yourself. For more details on financial aspects of the business, see Chapter 7.

Time Management

There will be times when working on multiple projects simultaneously can be stressful. What if you have three blog posts that are all due on the same day? What if you've sent out a proposal to a warm prospect and need to follow up on the same day or risk losing the work to a competitor? And, while all that is going on, your accountant calls and needs to meet with you about clarifying some expenses. How do you handle everything?

You will need to prioritize these items and determine what you absolutely must accomplish today. In many cases, the amount we think we *have to* do and what we actually *must* do are quite different. Generally, try to think in terms of three main categories: 1) paid work for a client; 2) proposals and marketing to get more work; and 3) managing your business. Some things can get diverted, such as the accountant's inquiry. A quick call or email to postpone the discussion to the next day will solve that. And, if you're working on several blog posts at the same time, stop and ask yourself a few questions: Do they all really get posted on the same day, or do you simply have to have a draft done for someone to approve that you can post tomorrow? What flexibility is there in this schedule? For the proposal that you're preparing, when did you promise to submit a quote?

Once you have things listed in order of priority, get to work. You may surprise yourself at how quickly you can get a job done when you are head down and focused. Make sure your distractions (email, phone, kids—you know what they are) are removed from the situation. Tackle the most important item first, then the second, and so on. Don't get caught in the trap of handling the small, easy, and quick items, just so you can tick them off your To Do list. You may find at the end of a day that you've done a dozen small, meaningless tasks, when you really needed to focus on one important job. Learn to know the difference.

Handling Job-Related Stress

You will discover that writing jobs come in waves. It is unlikely that your work will present itself in a nice orderly fashion from week to week (unless you focus strictly on doing regularly scheduled blogs or social monthly newsletters). There have been many times when I've quoted several jobs that are months apart only to have them all start at the same time. Advanced scheduling can solve some of this problem, but clear communication with each party involved is critical. If a customer that you quoted three months ago suddenly decides to do the job now, make it clear to them that you are currently working on other projects as well, and that this will alter the delivery schedule. Clients are usually more than happy to work with deadline changes if you communicate clearly and honestly. If you find this happening often, take a look at how much time you estimate to complete a project, and increase your estimate. It's always better to overestimate the amount of time it will take to do a job and deliver early, than to promise something in an impossible amount of time and deliver late. Do what you say you will do.

Asking for Help

There will be times as your business and reputation grow that you will have more work assignments than you can effectively manage on your own. What do you do if you have more requests for work than you can accommodate? This might sound scary, but it is a good thing. It means that you've reached a point where your skills and service have become known, and people want you to give them your best work. Perhaps it's time to consider growing your business. Chapter 10 will cover more about how to manage the growth of your business.

You've made the decision to start a business, and in so doing, you've made a commitment to its success. Communicating this clearly to those close to you will help everyone respect your goal of getting your business off the ground. You may be surprised at how much their support will help you stay focused. Find the tools you need to manage your time, make sure your calendar is always up to date, and don't take on more than you can handle.

Chapter 7: Finances

The financial aspects of your business are the indicators that show how you are doing. If your bottom line gets progressively larger, then you are going in the right direction. If you don't know what your bottom line is, then you could be headed for disaster faster than you think!

This chapter will share the basic concepts you need to understand about finance when starting your writing business. I am not an accountant or financial adviser and do not claim expertise in these fields. In fact, I strongly recommend that you look into hiring a financial professional who will help keep you on the right track. Here, I will share what methods I used that worked for me and will most likely work for you as well.

There are a number of financial considerations, but the two fundamental ones are money coming in and money going out. To stay in the "black," the amount of money coming in needs to be more than the amount of money going out. Sounds pretty simple, right? Your commitment needs to be to accurately record all the comings and goings of your money.

Quick Books or Simply Accounting

Although you can most likely manage your financial tracking with a simple spreadsheet program, using a program designed specifically for small business accounting is highly recommended. There are many simple and user-friendly software programs available to help you manage your books. Two of the most popular are *Quick Books* and *Simply Accounting*. Either program can be easily installed on your computer, and their online tutorials and help will answer any questions you may have when setting up.

The use of such programs not only allows you to record your income and expenses, but also offers a wide variety of reports that will prove useful as you develop your business. You can keep track of all your vendors and customers, with the option of printing a number of reports to tell you where you spend your money or who isn't paying you on time. As well, you can find out where you are spending most of your money and which types of services generate the most revenue. There are also several reports that may prove useful to your accountant when you are preparing your taxes.

Expenses and Receipts

When you decide to start your own business, people will tell you that you can write off everything. Well, you can't. There are many advantages to being able to take certain deductions on your tax return, but not every expense you've ever had is eligible for deduction. To illustrate, if you run a home-based business, a portion of certain expenses, such as heat, insurance, and maintenance, are eligible for deduction; however, this is based on the amount of space in your home used by your business as a percentage of your home's square footage. For example, if your office takes up 100 square feet and your home is a total of 1200 square feet, you can claim 8.3 percent of your heating bill for office use. There are some stipulations if you use part of your home for both personal and business use, so check the rules to be sure about what is truly eligible. This is where your accountant is invaluable.

You can use these links to view the Canada Revenue Agency website and learn more about eligible expense deductions for your business:

http://www.cra-arc.gc.ca/tx/bsnss/tpcs/slprtnr/bsnssxpnss/menu-eng.html

http://www.cra-arc.gc.ca/tx/bsnss/tpcs/slprtnr/rprtng/t2125/ln9945-eng.html

In addition to household expenses, you will be collecting receipts for various purchases you make through the course of doing business. There will be receipts for office supplies, computer repairs, or fuel for your vehicle so you can visit a client. Your best bet is to keep all receipts in one central spot. This makes them easily accessible when it's time to enter them into your accounting program. In the early days, I put all receipts into one manila envelope. At the end of the year, I tallied them all up, categorized them, and put them into a spreadsheet, and this is what I attached to my tax return as I was doing them myself. A word to the wise—keep your expenses to a minimum. You don't need a state-of-the-art computer, laser printer, and fancy stationary right out of the gate.

Over the course of the past dozen years, I've modified my record-keeping method so that now I keep all receipts in a running file, and at the end of the month I transfer them to a separate file labelled for that month. I go through these and discard the irrelevant ones, and then bring this file to a bookkeeper. She then inputs the receipts into an accounting program. We work together to ensure all the household bills that need partial entry are put in there, as well as for accuracy when year-end rolls around. At that point, a report is printed out listing the breakdown of expenses, and this is brought to my accountant to process the annual tax return.

Keep a running log of your activities in a Day-timer or calendar. This will come in handy when you are calculating such things as mileage, and you want to cross-reference your activities to ensure what you had recorded is indeed accurate. This sort of backup record can prove useful if you are ever audited.

Income and Invoices

On the happy side of the financial equation is recording your income. The same computer program is used to generate invoices to your customers when you do a job. Each business is different, but I generally recommend invoicing a deposit amount for new clients or large projects, and then billing on pre-agreed dates thereafter.

Setting up a schedule for your invoicing tasks will make your life easier. For example, if there are clients that you work with on a regular basis, set aside the last day of the month to invoice them (or invoice on the 15th and 30th of each month). If you are working on several projects simultaneously, choose one day a week to review what needs to be invoiced and add that to your schedule. Forgetting to invoice or waiting until weeks after the project is complete does not add to your bottom line and is sloppy business practice. Establishing a routine early on will save you grief and aggravation later.

What Will You Charge?

Figuring out what to charge a client can be difficult. Over the years, the amount I've invoiced for an article has varied from $50 to $350. So much depends on your level of experience and knowledge of the subject, as well as what the market will bear and the type of company you are doing it for. Your regular rate might be $250 for an article, but if a small business owner in an interesting niche market wants you to write one for $50, will you do it? You may really want to learn more about the topic and have it as part of your portfolio. You may be too busy to be able to accommodate him (or too slow to turn down the offer). Setting rates is a challenging task and is quite often a moving target. Researching realistic rates is a good first step. Contact associations or writers' groups and ask what the going rate is for the type of writing projects you plan on doing.

The most effective strategy is to establish a price range for a certain type of project, such as a blog post, website, newsletter, or article, and outline to the client what factors come under consideration when you calculate the rate. Learn how to negotiate and be certain of your bottom line. There will always be a point at which you are willing to walk away. Cheapening yourself by constantly cutting your prices does not make you look better in the eyes of the client—quite the contrary, in fact. If you think so little of your services to barely charge anything, then the client may not think they are getting the quality they demand. Keep in mind the value that the client will receive from the service you provide. For example, if your compelling direct mail copy results in thousands of dollars of added revenue for them, then a few hundred dollars to pay for the copy isn't very much, is it? See Chapter 7 Notes in Appendix A for a web link that offers some very useful negotiation strategies.

Collection Strategies

I am happy to say that I've never had to write off any invoice due to lack of payment. I have, however, chased a client for a full year to get paid for an overdue invoice. What do you do if faced with a client who won't pay?

Let's back up a minute. Before you even get to the invoicing stage, you will have gone through a number of other steps first. Initially, your contact with the client will be a discussion of the project in detail. Your first job is to create a comprehensive quote or estimate that outlines the project, *as you understand it*. This is very important. There is nothing worse than the client thinking he asked for one thing, and then you deliver something completely different. Your quote should detail how you intend to deliver on what is required, including partial deliverables and completion date. It will also outline how you intend to invoice. For example, you may invoice one-third as a deposit, and once that is paid, the project will commence. Halfway through completion, you will invoice a second third, and the final third will be invoiced upon completion. Ensure that you list the number of revisions or changes you will include in the price, as well as your terms of payment. Also include the interest charges you will add to the total, should the client be late in paying. Have your customer sign the quote when you start so that they acknowledge having read and agreed to your proposal. Taking these steps will ensure that you are both clear on what is expected and when it is expected by. No confusion. This will then give you leverage if the client decides not to pay or is very late in paying.

Ongoing Contracts

When working with a client on projects that are ongoing, it is wise to draw up an agreement or contract that outlines how you will proceed. Include details such as what tasks will be performed, how many hours are to be dedicated to the project, how you will account for your time, how often you will invoice, your payment terms, and deadlines for everything. Include in the contract a duration and point at which the agreement will be reviewed. I recommend reviewing your agreements every three months to be sure you are still satisfying the client's needs, and they are not attempting to load you with additional tasks that were not included in the original agreement. Clear and honest communication is critical to achieve an amicable and desired outcome.

Managing the finances of your business does not mean you have to have an accounting degree. Common sense record keeping is straightforward especially if you have the tools you need and consistently dedicate time to the task. Staying on top of your money matters means you can make adjustments to correct problems before they get out of hand. (See Appendix B for sample income statement and cash flow templates.)

Chapter 8: Marketing

Once you've decided what type of writing you are going to do and who your target customers will be, your next important step is to get the message out to your target audience that you are in business. There are several marketing strategies you can employ. Some will be more effective than others, and many are low cost or no cost. Try to do as much as you can with "sweat equity" (that is, free) when first starting out. The key is to develop a variety of marketing tools and platforms to reach your target audience in all the places where they might be.

Establish Your Brand

You will want to create a professional image for your new business as you get ready to launch. There are some things you can do yourself, and other things that will require outside help. At the very least, consult with a professional designer to create your logo. Discuss with them what your business is about, and ask them to help you create a professional image. Don't rush through this. Take the time to develop something you can be proud of.

Website

Among the first things you should do to market yourself is to create a professional website. With the widely available content management systems and open source products on the market, it is relatively easy to set up a website. If you have some technical acumen and no budget, take the time to learn one of the platforms, such as Wordpress, Dot Net Nuke, or Joomla. They are straightforward to use with a minimum of programming. (See the description in Chapter 5, and Chapter 5 Notes in Appendix A on how to make a website). If you are not comfortable with setting up your own website, there are many skilled web professionals who can be hired for a wide range of fees. Hiring a web developer has its advantages since they will likely include basic search engine optimization

(SEO), as well as suggestions based on your specific needs. All this is designed to get more traffic to your website.

Blog

As part of your website, you can develop a blog. This is an ideal place to talk about the comings and goings of your company. It is also where you will post information of interest to your readers, perhaps answering their questions or offering solutions to problem situations. A blog requires commitment, however, so only start it if you plan to stay with it. There is nothing worse than discovering a new blog, and then having the author not post for weeks. There is no hard and fast rule on this, but it has been suggested that to keep people interested, you will need to post at least once a week, or three times a week to have any real impact. Search engines will look at your blog with greater interest if there are frequent and consistent updates.

Marketing Plan and Strategy

Much like a business plan, a marketing plan can be as complex or as simple as you like (see Appendix B for a sample marketing plan table of contents). The focus is on whom you will reach out to and how you plan on doing it. One of the greatest marketing philosophies I've come across is from Susan Carter of www.writerprofits.com. (See Chapter 8 Notes in Appendix A for a link to Susan Carter's 7-step marketing plan for writers.) She suggests that you create a repeatable marketing strategy. In other words, come up with two or three tactics that you actually enjoy doing, such as email blasts, determine the time frame under which you will do them, and then get to work. For example, if you have a 40 percent open rate for your email blasts (this is the number of recipients who actually open the email; 40 percent is considered good), then set a regular schedule and send out email blasts with a marketing focus. Consistency is key because people will need to see your message or brand several times before they've actually built up enough trust to call you and hire you. Also, the timing of the message needs to be right for the person receiving

53

it. If they aren't ready to buy, they just aren't ready to buy. This is why you need to send your message regularly to keep you and your business offerings "top of mind."

Marketing Collateral

When starting out, you will want the message about the services you offer to reach as many people as possible, which means you'll be distributing non-digital materials. Helpful tools include a business card, a brochure or flyer, and perhaps a direct mail piece. There are templates and tools you can use that are already on your computer, such as MS Word, but you may wish to contact a graphic designer to help you develop these marketing materials. Online services such as Vistaprint are a good place to start, to show you the wide variety of options available.

Social Media

There are a number of social media platforms that can help you get "out there" and connect with people online. Be selective in choosing which platforms you will participate in, and set up a profile. Recommended platforms for you to start with are LinkedIn, Facebook, Twitter, and Google Plus). Here are some of my observations on how these social media platforms might be useful for your business.

What Can LinkedIn Do for My Company?

LinkedIn is a platform designed to connect professionals, and you will likely see people there that you've worked with. Setting up a LinkedIn profile will enable you to outline your experience, as well as describe the services you offer. You can set up both a personal profile page and a business page. I recommend doing both.

LinkedIn is referred to as the "world's largest professional network" and is particularly useful for business-to-business organizations. It's a tool that lets you keep tabs on what your business contacts are doing, search for professional services and products, participate in groups, buy targeted ads, get recommendations from customers and colleagues, and research potential customers and competitors.

LinkedIn offers a platform where you can network and keep in touch with contacts. If there is a former colleague you haven't heard from in a while, going on LinkedIn to find out where they are and sending a message is a great opportunity to reconnect.

LinkedIn is often the first place that businesses go to seek professional services such as copywriters. It makes sense to have your profile and company page optimized with the appropriate keywords so that you are found more easily.

What Can Facebook Do for My Company?

I initially used Facebook only for personal connections with family and friends. I have since gone on to build a business page for my writing company where I can create messages and share links specific to my target audience.

I admit to not being that active on Facebook. My Facebook "page" consists of several pages together, which make a mini-website with the same look and feel as my actual website. I share interesting links or ideas, but, for the most part, I consider Facebook to be more valuable if you are operating a Business-to-Consumer (B2C) business. My primary reason for maintaining a Facebook page is to illustrate to prospects and clients what they can do with Facebook to broaden their network. At the very least, if you are consulting with someone on how to market themselves more effectively (and hence hire you to create the marketing communications), then you must understand how and why Facebook is a valuable tool.

What Can Twitter Do for My Company?

When I first heard about Twitter, I simply didn't get it. I could not understand why people would waste their time writing tiny little messages to people they didn't know. Eventually, I started to connect

55

with people who had similar interests to mine. I followed experts in my field and professionals who owned businesses that I admired. I checked out news and celebrity offerings to offset all the business connections. I remember finding one person who was taking a year and communicating only using social media. I thought it was an interesting exercise, and we tweeted back and forth a few times. It just seemed amazing to me that a total stranger doing something unusual ended up talking back to me from his farm on the east coast. If he ends up writing a book about the experience, I'll buy it.

One of the things I enjoy about Twitter is the links that people share. I've been learning SEO tips for years, and in order to keep up with the ever-changing industry, there are some experts I like to follow such as Search Engine Watch. The links they provide (which are usually links to their well-written blog) help keep me up to speed on the latest and greatest in the search industry.

Of course, it is easy to get distracted on Twitter (as with any social platform!), so I usually give myself a specific amount of time to read and post tweets, after which it gets turned off. I then may tweet periodically during the day if something interesting is happening. I also like to share inspirational quotes, which aren't time sensitive, so I schedule those using such tools as HootSuite (www.hootsuite.com) or Buffer (www.bufferapp.com).

What Can Google Plus Do for My Company?

Many believe that Google Plus was a little late to the game and will never catch up with Facebook in popularity. While that may be true, the platform does offer a different and compelling user experience worth checking out. Chris Brogan has written an excellent book on the subject of using Google Plus for business, which provides quite a few tips and techniques for using the platform. It has been proven that having an authoritative Google Plus page will help you rank higher in search results.

The communities and hangouts are fun features that set the platform apart from the others. You can invite people to "hang out," and have a video chat with up to ten people at a time from anywhere in the world. The community feature is ideal if you want to keep messages, posts, and information shared between a select few people. One of my favourite websites, Social Media Examiner, offers in-depth examples of how to use Google Plus (see Chapter 8 Notes in Appendix A for Social Media Examiner's link to how to grow your Google Plus engagement).

Market Research

Once you've set up an online presence, you will want to do a little digging to see exactly who you will be targeting to get some business. Going back to your list of services, whatever you are planning to offer will determine where you will look for business. In Chapter 5, we discussed how to find businesses through the use of directories, library searches, and online searches. It also makes sense to reach out to your local chamber of commerce for businesses in your area, or consider becoming a member to take advantage of networking and business opportunities. Check into national associations as well. You may be able to access their membership lists by becoming a member, but be cautious not to become an annoying salesman to your fellow members. You wouldn't like to be treated that way.

In addition to researching who will purchase your service, take the time to research your competition. Who else in your area is offering the same or similar services? Check creative services directories and professional associations to try and get more information about the competition. Find out how long they've been in business and what sets you apart from them. Or, if you offer something similar, perhaps reaching out to them makes sense. I have often collaborated with other writers, or we've passed on work to each other if our schedules are backed up.

Networking

One of the best ways to market your business is through networking. People do business with people, not with websites and brochures. Looking someone in the eye and shaking their hand can mean the difference between being hired or being passed over for the competition. Chapter 9 will examine the importance of in-person networking to the success of your writing business.

Chapter 9: Networking

There are basically two types of networking: virtual networking and in-person networking. There are plenty of groups you can join online that will give you the opportunity to have conversations with others. Most social media platforms fall into this category. In this chapter, the focus is on physical networking.

Why Network?

As a sole proprietor with a writing business, much of your day will be spent alone in front of a computer. There are not a lot of chances to meet other people, particularly potential clients, if you spend *all* of your time there. You'll need to get yourself out into the world if you want to make a go of it.

There are many reasons for networking, and not all of them revolve around your business. By getting out and placing yourself in new situations, you are expanding your circle by meeting new people and learning more about the world around you. For your business, networking can lead to new job opportunities, client leads, partnerships, and mentors. Getting connected with others means your name will come to mind when someone remembers that dynamic writer they met at a networking event. Meeting strangers can help you polish your image and be clear about what your goals are. It takes guts to walk into a room full of strangers, so networking is definitely a character-building pursuit.

How to Get Started Networking

One of the best ways to start networking is to join a group or association relevant to your business. The first organization I joined was the local chamber of commerce. They offered opportunities to volunteer and to meet other member companies. They host a wide variety of events that are geared to educating members, as well as providing opportunities for networking and engagement. Links to my website are posted on their website, and they keep their membership informed with a weekly newsletter. The website and newsletter also offer advertising opportunities to help me grow my business.

I had also found a local communications group, the Halton Peel Communications Association (HPCA), and when I first walked into a room with these people, it was like coming home. For the first time, I felt that I was among people who understood what I was about and what I was trying to accomplish because they were in the same situation. The membership includes writers, graphic designers, photographers, web developers, marketing specialists, videographers, and more. Not only are we able to discuss common issues that we experience as entrepreneurs, but we are also in a position to collaborate on projects, thereby broadening the scope of jobs we can quote on.

Check your local business community for business networking groups such as a regional BNI group (see Chapter 9 Notes in Appendix A for links to BNI Canada and other business networking groups).

Tap Your Network to Grow Business

The primary reason you join a networking group is to get contacts and referrals. But it goes beyond that. Becoming part of such a group means that you are developing relationships with a pool of diversely skilled individuals. This becomes a valuable resource that you can tap into and gain valuable information from. Asking for advice from, or offering advice to, your fellow members helps the entire group to grow. Just remember not to cross the line by asking for too much free advice. It is acceptable to ask one or two questions, but don't expect people to give away for free what they would usually charge for.

Top 10 Networking Tips

People are often uncomfortable networking because they feel they need to act differently than they normally do. One of the keys to effective networking is to be genuine. Behave like yourself, not a pumped-up facsimile trying to get business. Here are ten suggestions for your next networking event:

1. **Help Other People** – Look for ways to help others, rather than to see what you can get out of people. Any relationship goes two ways, and the best way to start off is to offer your service. The more value you create for others, the more it will come back to you.

2. **Ask Questions** – And listen to the answers. Genuine interest in what others are doing is a good first step in establishing a rapport with someone. Keep it simple and start with questions such as, "May I join you?" "What brings you to this event?"

3. **Be Selective** – Take the time to determine who in the room may provide a service that is relevant to you. Strike up meaningful conversations with a few people, rather than trying to "power network" and get your business card into everyone's hands.

4. **Reduce Expectations** – If you go to a networking event expecting to meet a lot of new potential clients, you are jumping the gun. Learn about people first and find out what makes them interesting. Ditch the sales pitch.

5. **Broaden Your Scope** – Reach out to people outside your industry. Getting to know professionals in a variety of disciplines will expand your network in unexpected ways. Don't underestimate how valuable a new contact might be. You don't know who they know—yet!

6. **Show Up Early** – As an earlier arrival, you'll notice it's quieter, and people won't have settled into groups or found conversation partners yet.

7. **Share Your Passion** – Enthusiasm is often contagious. There's a reason you got into this business; share your excitement with others. It will likely inspire them to share their passion as well, making for a memorable conversation for you both.

8. **Don't Hijack the Conversation** – Successful networkers are very good at making people feel special. Look people in the eye, repeat their name, listen to what they have to say, and suggest topics that are easy to discuss. Be a conversationalist, not a talker.

9. **Remember to Follow Up –** This may be the most important point of all. If you've had an interesting conversation with someone, ask what is the best way to stay in touch. Whether by email, phone, or LinkedIn, make sure you follow up within 48 hours to show you're interested, and make reference to something you talked about so they remember you.

10. **Nurture Your Current Network –** Networking is not just about meeting new people; it's also about keeping in contact with your existing network.

While looking for perspectives on how to network, I turned to one of my LinkedIn groups for inspiration. Here are some thoughts they shared:

"Productive networking is an art. Many people migrate to people they already know and go for the 'safe' networking. Gone are the days of 'selling' networking. Networking these days is about building relationships, and I believe the most successful approach is to network with the intent of finding out how you can help / connect others. Doing this at a networking event is often not enough and needs to be followed up with a coffee. In terms of 'breaking the ice,' many other people are just as nervous or have been in your shoes before, so just ask people how they are, how their week has been, and go from there—don't be afraid to talk about things other than business."

"I teach our advisors the art of building a referral network. At networking events, the important thing is to find people who would make good referral partners for you, meaning that you can provide significant value add to their business. It is definitely not about your business at the event. In fact, I tell my new advisors who are not used to networking to leave their cards at home. This is a reminder that it is not about them; it's about the business of the person they are talking to. Also, you must fully engage the person you are chatting with at a networking event. It is easy to get distracted by other people you may know or by someone who seems more interesting. I try to explain that it is not even business that you are trying to gain at such events. It is really business partners or people that are willing to open their network to your services. People will only do that once they know, like, and trust you. And that requires a full understanding of their business."

Do you notice a consistent theme? With any networking event, don't go in thinking about what you can get out of it. Go to the event with the mindset that you are there to start, build, and nurture relationships. You know that people you've connected with become people that you trust, and they are likely the first ones you will call when the need arises. Be one of those people.

Chapter 10: Growing Your Business

In Chapter 6, we asked, "What do you do if you have more requests for work than you can accommodate?" There really are two ways to handle this. You can say "no" and divert the client to a competitor, or you can say "yes" and find someone to do the work.

If you say "no," the odds are pretty good that you've lost that client. They'll use someone else, be satisfied, and it will be much harder to win that client the next time (unless, of course, they are dissatisfied, in which case you may still have another chance).

If you say "yes" and commit to doing the work, how will you make it happen? You've already determined that you can't do it yourself, so who do you trust to get the work done? Ideally, you will have prepared for this scenario by reaching out in advance to several writers in your network, and pre-arranged how to handle a referral opportunity. They may agree to subcontract the project from you so that the client only has to deal with you. They may insist on billing through their own company and may agree to a "finder's fee" or commission. Whatever arrangement works for you is fine, but spell it out in advance of an actual client request, and write down the terms so everyone is clear. Setting up this type of arrangement is an ideal way to expand your service offerings. Finding another writer who specializes in something you haven't offered before means you can appeal to a broader customer base.

Depending on the project, it may be possible for you to outsource a part of it. For example, you can find a research assistant online or through your network. This person can do the legwork to assemble ten key points on a topic you request. You can then take that information and craft a blog post.

Building Your Team

As your days fill with writing work, you will find yourself more pressed for time to manage other areas of your business. You can easily outsource administrative tasks such as bookkeeping to competent professionals who will do the job quickly and well, freeing you up to work on client projects. Virtual Assistants (VAs) are multi-talented professionals who offer a variety of services based on your needs, including the preparation of spreadsheets or Powerpoint presentations. The VA I work with most closely not only excels at the administrative tasks I need help with, but she is also a social media specialist. She picks up the slack and has taught me a great deal. Having a skilled VA on my team has given me the confidence to try new things and reminds me to put effort into my business.

With regards to sourcing subcontractors online, sites such as odesk (www.odesk.com) are often met with mixed reviews. Some writers fear that they can't compete with the writers found on odesk who are willing to write a 500-word blog post for $5. If someone wants to pay $5 for a blog post, it is fairly certain that they will get a blog post worth no more than $5. None of my clients would tolerate that level of quality. If, however, I hire someone for $5 to provide me with ten relevant facts on a technical topic, that's a different story. I can then take those facts and craft a blog post written in the voice and style expected by the client. The skill and experience I bring to the project are worth more than $5, and my customer is happy to pay my fee and work with me to produce a quality blog post.

The bottom line is to use due diligence when seeking a subcontractor online. Ask a lot of questions and insist upon seeing examples of their past work. And, of course, only pay when the work is completed as promised and to your specifications. With proper management, sourcing subcontractors online can be a viable addition to your business plan.

Expanding Your Offerings: Selling Products

You may reach the point where you begin to realize that there are only so many hours in a day for you to write, and that creates a ceiling for your income. That isn't necessarily the case. You can create information products such as eBooks or special reports that can be used to add to your subscriber list or that you can sell. This can produce a revenue stream that is not directly tied to the number of hours you're working. You may wish to create training materials and conduct online webinars, which could also provide an alternative source of income. The advantage of this, of course, is that you create the materials once, yet they are purchased over and over again.

If you choose to develop products, do some research on what is out there on your topic and see if there is a focus that hasn't been tried before. You will likely notice that on some topics such as blogging, there is an overabundance of websites, eBooks, and courses that you can buy to help you blog better. Does that mean the market is saturated? Well, maybe. But it could also be an indication that this is a hot topic that people are hungry for, and that you may have a new and interesting twist to help them be successful. If that's the case, go ahead and write the book! When I decided to write this book, my first thought was that there must be a dozen titles just like mine. It's such a common topic, right? Well, there was only one. And although I read that book, it had a completely different tone and focus than this book. I wanted my book to be a simple, no-nonsense primer designed to help anyone get a writing business up and going.

Become a Teacher

With experience under your belt, you may feel that you'd like to share with others the knowledge you've gained that has led to your success. You may consider offering a webinar series or online course to teach groups of people about what you do. Much like writing an eBook, when you develop a webinar series, you can create it once (with regular updates so the material doesn't get dated) and offer it to many people over and over again. One key consideration when developing a webinar is that you will be dependent on technology to share your material. When the time comes, you'll want to have backups and redundancies so that if something goes terribly wrong, you can make a few adjustments and get right back on track. People are tolerant of the occasional glitch, but if there is a high-pitched hum coming from your microphone, you'll be issuing a *lot* of refunds. You'll also need to have some personality and presentation skills, so if you are extremely shy and faint at the idea of speaking in front of others, this might not be for you.

Mentoring and coaching services are other alternate ways to offer your teaching skills. This usually brings you back to the hourly rate, but it would be a limited and exclusive opportunity, meaning your charge for these unique services would be higher.

Growing your business should happen gradually. Trying to be everything to everyone is a one-way ticket to a meltdown. There are only so many hours you want to be working in a day, and the rest of the time you have other pursuits. Figure out how to get the work done by building your team and enhancing your service offerings. If you're still inundated with work after that, congratulations! It means you've started and grown a successful writing business.

Appendix A

Chapter Notes

Chapter 1 Notes

Peter Bowerman. *The Well-Fed Writer*. Atlanta, GA: Fanove Publishing, 2000.

Chapter 2 Notes

Exercise at Your Desk:

Sitting for extended periods can cause back pain, poor posture, leg cramps, and boredom. There are exercises you can do at your desk to improve flexibility and strength such as stretching, muscle strengthening, and short stints of aerobic exercises.

Here are a few stretches and aerobic moves to try between tasks:

- Neck stretch: Touch your ear to your shoulder and hold it there.
- Chest opener: Stretch your arms back as if you were trying to grab a pencil between your shoulder blades.
- Back extensions: Hold your hips and gently extend your back by bending backwards.
- Wrist/arm stretch: Stand at your desk and with arms straight, place your palms on your desk with your fingers pointed toward you. Lower your body slowly until you feel the stretch. Hold for 15 seconds.
- Lower-body strengthening: Sit in your chair. Extend one leg out straight in front of you. Hold for 2 seconds. Then raise it up as high as you can and hold again for 2 seconds. Repeat with each leg 15 times.
- Jumping Jacks: Jump up raising your arms above your head and spreading your legs. Jump again, bringing legs together and arms down to your sides. Repeat 15 times.
- Run or march in place for 60 seconds.
- Football-drill: While seated, pump both arms over your head for 30 seconds, then rapidly tap your feet on the floor for 30 seconds. Repeat 3–5 times.
- Lunges: With hands on your hips, step forward with your right leg and bend your left knee until almost touching the floor. Step back into the starting position. Step forward with your left leg and bend your right knee until almost touching the floor. Alternate, doing 5 lunges per side.

Give yourself a head start by setting up your chair at the proper height to reduce strain on your neck and back. Adjust the height so you're in a 90-90-90 position; feet flat on the floor and your knees and hips bent at 90-degree angles. Keep your lower spine flat against the back of the chair to maintain proper curvature. This will help decrease your chance of hunching forward, which causes spasms in the back and neck.

Computer information source: http://bluecapra.com/business-laptop/

Check out this link for some analysis of best computer buys:
http://www.techradar.com/news/computing/best-computer-how-to-choose-the-right-one-935053

Chapter 3 Notes

Registering your business (Service Ontario): Go here to search, register, or renew your business, and to get a Master Business Licence:
https://www.appmybizaccount.gov.on.ca/sodp/portal/osb

Registering for HST: http://www.cra-arc.gc.ca/tx/bsnss/tpcs/bn-ne/bro-ide/rstrctns/menu-eng.html

Record Keeping: http://www.cra-arc.gc.ca/tx/bsnss/tpcs/slprtnr/rcrds/menu-eng.html

Guide to Market Research and Analysis (Canada Business Network):
http://www.canadabusiness.ca/eng/page/2691/

Business Plan Template: http://office.microsoft.com/en-ca/templates/business-plan-for-startup-business-TC001017520.aspx

Chapter 4 Notes

For many years, the tool I used was Manymoon, which enabled me not only to track tasks and projects, but to create timesheets for each project so I could accurately track time. Just before starting this book, Manymoon became Do.com and they no longer offered the time-tracking feature. I then searched for alternatives and have begun using Asana (www.asana.com) for project tracking and Toggl (www.toggl.com) for time tracking. What would you recommend?

Email Marketing Programs: www.mailchimp.com;
www.constantcontact.com

Keyword Suggestion Tools:

Google Keyword suggestion tool is now only available when you set up an Adwords account. Alternate keyword suggestion tools can be found at www.keywordeye.com, www.soovle.com, and www.freshkey.com. You may also want to try Wordtracker at https://freekeywords.wordtracker.com/

Chapter 5 Notes

How to Build a Website:

1. *Select and Register a Domain*: This is what you see after "www" in the web browser and that will appear after the "@" in your email address. Take care when selecting your domain name. It should describe what your website is about or be a catchy name. Try to keep it simple and not too long, and, if possible, use ".com." There are many online options for registering a domain name, but you may wish to register the domain with the same place where you register your web hosting.

2. *Choose a Website Hosting Supplier*: A website host stores your website files so that they can be viewable on the Internet. You will usually pay for hosting fees annually, and you pay up front. I prefer www.bluehost.com. They offer a free domain name when you register for hosting. They also offer a user-friendly and comprehensive dashboard to manage your account. Bluehost also includes the option for hosting multiple domains with one hosting account. (Please note that there are many web hosting providers online and of the few I've tried, Bluehost had the functionality and usability features that appealed to me. You may want to shop around.)

3. *Building Your Website*: There are many options when it comes to building a website. If you have already built website files on your computer, you can upload it to the Bluehost servers and manage your site there. If starting from scratch, you can build a website on Wordpress (wordpress.org). This site provides detailed instructions that walk you through the process. You will also be able to create a new email account associated with your website.

Charity Village List of Charities:
https://charityvillage.com/directories/organizations-a-h.aspx

Suggested Cold-Calling Script/Intro Email Format:

1. Give a very brief introduction of who you are.

2. Mention what you know about the prospect and the issues they face (you'll need to do some pre-call research).

3. Tell the prospect the ideas you have on how to improve these issues or the prospect's business in general (again, do your research and come up with some ideas before making the call).

4. Put some proof behind your ideas by mentioning whom you have helped solve similar issues.

5. Thank the prospect and let them know you'll be following up.

Online Writing Job Sites:
www.freelancewritinggigs.com
www.problogger.net
www.poewar.com
www.bloggerjobs.biz
www.mediabistro.com
www.freelanceswitch.com

www.sunoasis.com

www.journalismjobs.com

www.allfreelancewritingjobs.com

www.wahm.com

www.online-writing-jobs.com

www.sologig.com

www.Gofreelance.com

www.freelancewriting.com

www.indeed.com

www.worldwidefreelance.com

www.3to30.com

www.fileply.com

www.leavingworkbehind.com

Chapter 7 Notes

Tips on how to negotiate effectively:
http://www.inc.com/magazine/20101101/how-to-negotiate-effectively.html

Chapter 8 Notes

Susan Carter's 7-step marketing plan for writers:
http://www.writerprofits.com/the-7-step-marketing-plan-for-writers/

In-depth examples of how to grow your Google Plus engagement:
http://www.socialmediaexaminer.com/tag/google-plus/

Chapter 9 Notes

Business Networking Groups:
BNI Canada – A networking group that offers a structured and supported word of mouth marketing program with a proven track record of helping members increase their competitive edge.

Black Card Events – An association whose mission is to provide professionals with an opportunity to expand their business network through events where like-minded individuals come together.

BPA Canada – A professional referral association whose main purpose is to give its members quality referrals while helping members build their client relationships.

Canadian Association of Women Executives & Entrepreneurs (CAWEE) – A not-for-profit, member-run association that connects businesswomen. CAWEE focuses on relationship networking between professionals that are interested in helping build other members' businesses and "paying it forward."

Progressive Group for Independent Business (BNRC) – A networking group that offers opportunities to grow your business and continually require members to share contacts.

Young Entrepreneurs Association (YEA) – A non-profit member organization whose mandate is to support young people in business to learn and receive peer support and mentorship. Aimed at business owners 35 and under.

Appendix B

Templates and Samples

Chapter 3

Business Plan Table of Contents Sample

Business Plan Table of Contents

WHAT ARE MY COMPETITORS' STRENGTHS AND WEAKNESSES?

Name of business:

	Strength	Weakness
Customers		
Location		
Website appearance		
Range of products or services		
Quality of product or service		
Price of product or service		
Unique aspects of product or service		
Reputation		
Quality of staff		
Marketing		

Its main strengths are

Its main weaknesses are

Chapter 5

Customer Identification Worksheet

WHO WILL BUY MY SERVICE?

Service or Product:

Characteristics of possible customers	Male	Female
Age Range		
Business / occupation		
Geographic location		
Sales / Income level		
Purchasing habits		

The following people / businesses are most likely to buy this product or service from me:

Chapter 7

Income Statement Template

MY WRITING BUSINESS
Income Statement for the Year Ended (Date)

SALES		
	Writing Services	$ xxxx
	Project Management	$ xxxx
TOTAL SALES		$ xxxx
EXPENSES		
	Advertising and Promotion	$ xxx
	Depreciation, equipment	$ xxx
	Electricity	$ xxx
	Insurance	$ xxx
	Interest and bank charges	$ xxx
	Maintenance and repairs	$ xxx
	Professional fees	$ xxx
	Office supplies	$ xxx
	Telephone and Utilities	$ xxx

	Vehicle and travel expenses	$ xxx
TOTAL EXPENSES		$ xxxx
NET INCOME	Total Sales – Total Expenses	$ xxxx

Download spreadsheet template at www.writerinc.ca

Chapter 7

Cash Flow Template

	JA	FE	...	NO	DE	TOTAL
Opening Cash Balance	$x	$x	$x	$x	$x	
RECEIPTS						
Cash received from sales						$xx
Cash from receivables						$xx
Loan proceeds						$xx
TOTAL RECEIPTS						$xx
DISBURSEMENTS						$xx
Accounts Payable						$xx
Subcontractor Fees						$xx
Supplies						$xx
Telephone & Utilities						$xx
Insurance						$xx

Advertising & PR						$xx
Maintenance						$xx
Taxes						$xx
Miscellaneous						$xx
TOTAL DISBURSEMENTS						$xx
SURPLUS / DEFICIT	$xx	$xx	$xx	$xx	$x	$xx

Download spreadsheet template at www.writerinc.ca

Chapter 8

Marketing Plan Table of Contents Sample

Marketing Plan Table of Contents

1.0 Executive Summary

2.0 Situation Analysis

      2.1 Corporate Summary

      2.2 Market Summary

      2.3 SWOTT Analysis

            2.3.1 Strengths

            2.3.2 Weaknesses

            2.3.3 Opportunities

            2.3.4 Threats

            2.3.5 Trends

      2.4 Competition

      2.5 Product/Service Offerings

      2.6 Channels of Distribution

3.0 Marketing Strategy

      3.1 Mission

      3.2 Marketing Goal and Objectives

      3.3 Financial Objectives of Business Plan

About The Author

Marnie Hughes started Communication Artistry over ten years ago and has developed the business to provide not only writing services, but also website consultation, project management, and online marketing services.

In addition to her passion for writing, Marnie supports the local business community as editor of the Chamber of Commerce quarterly newsletter, *BusinessLink*. Marnie is a married mother of three, a black belt in karate, and a volunteer with seniors in her community.

Connect with the author online:
Twitter: @marniehughes
Facebook: https://www.facebook.com/StartYourWritingBusiness
Website: http://writerinc.ca/

Printed in Great Britain
by Amazon.co.uk, Ltd.,
Marston Gate.